Zen Puppies

MEDITATIONS FOR THE WISE MINDS OF DOG LOVERS

Buddha
and the editors of
Mango Media

Cover Design: Roberto Núñez

Layout & Design: Roberto Núñez

For permission requests, please contact the publisher at:

Mango Publishing Group

2850 Douglas Road, 3rd Floor

Coral Gables, FL 33134 USA

info@mango.bz

For special orders, quantity sales, course adoptions and corporate sales, please email the publisher at sales@mango.bz. For trade and wholesale sales, please contact Ingram Publisher Services at customer.service@ingramcontent.com or +1.800.509.4887.

Zen Puppies: Meditations for the Wise Minds of Dog Lovers

Library of Congress Cataloging-in-Publication has been applied for.
ISBN: (paperback) 978-1-63353-718-7, (ebook) 978-1-63353-719-4
BISAC category code: REL092000 RELIGION / Buddhism / Zen

Printed in the United States of America

TABLE OF CONTENTS

MIND AND BODY 9

Verse 1: "But to satisfy the necessities of life..." 11
Verse 2: "An insincere and evil friend is more..." 12
Verse 3: "Be wise. Treat yourself, your mind..." 13
Verse 4: "By defilement of mind, beings are..." 14
Verse 5: "As long as the mind does not know..." 15
Verse 6: "To keep the body in good health is a..." 17
Verse 7: "Think with the whole body..." 18
Verse 8: "Do not lose yourself in the past..." 19
Verse 9: "Not the wind, not the flag; mind is..." 20
Verse 10: "Buddha means awareness, the..." 21
Verse 11: "Calming allows us to rest, and..." 23
Verse 12: "If you want to climb a mountain..." 24
Verse 13: "I come to realize that mind is no..." 25
Verse 14: "It is a man's own mind, not his..." 26
Verse 15: "If with a pure mind a person speaks..." 27
Verse 16: "When deluded, one is called an... " 29
Verse 17: "The way you do anything is the..." 30
Verse 18: "If you are unwilling to make efforts..." 31
Verse 19: "Control your eyes, ears, nose, body..." 32
Verse 20: "Pride and indifference shroud this..." 33
Verse 21: "Hell does not exist from its own side... " 35
Verse 22: "Like a fish taken from the water and..." 36
Verse 23: "Neither a mother, nor a father, nor..." 37
Verse 24: "One who has no wound on the hand..." 38
Verse 25: "Irrigators guide the water; fletchers..." 39
Verse 26: "Death carries off a person who is..." 41
Verse 27: "One who has learned little grows..." 42
Verse 28: "Those who, having broken free from..." 43
Verse 29: "Let right deeds be your motive, not..." 44
Verse 30: "Even so, an action to be done by body..." 45

HAPPINESS 47

Verse 31: "I do not dispute with the world; rather it is..." 49

Verse 32: "Better than a thousand useless words is one..." 50
Verse 33: "There is no way to happiness, happiness is..." 51
Verse 34: "We will develop and cultivate the liberation..." 52
Verse 35: "Health is the greatest gift, contentment is the..." 53
Verse 36: "The Buddha said, "Those who rejoice in..." 55
Verse 37: "He who is provided with forbearance and..." 56
Verse 38: "Acquisition is the root of suffering." 57
Verse 39: "Sometimes your joy is the source of your..." 58
Verse 40: "Everyone hears only what he understands." 59
Verse 41: "Letting go gives us freedom, and freedom is... " 61
Verse 42: "The ocean of suffering is immense, but if you... " 62
Verse 43: "If you understand, you will suffer less, and you... " 63
Verse 44: "You yourself must strive. The Buddhas only... " 64
Verse 45: "All those who suffer in the world do so because..." 65
Verse 46: "If a man does what is good, let him do it..." 67
Verse 47: "He who knows that all things are his mind..." 68
Verse 48: "They are happy indeed who own nothing at..." 69
Verse 49: "The one who walks in the company of fools..." 70
Verse 50: "There is no fire like passion, there is no evil..." 71
Verse 51: "We live happily indeed when we are not..." 73
Verse 52: "From pleasure comes grief, from pleasure..." 74
Verse 53: "Those who, seeking their own happiness..." 75
Verse 54: "Mules are good if trained, and so are noble..." 76
Verse 55: "Be not thoughtless, watch your thoughts..." 77
Verse 56: "But whoever overcomes this fierce..." 79
Verse 57: "Those who are slaves to passion follow..." 80
Verse 58: "No, a deed is well done if one does..." 81
Verse 59: "The good renounce everything..." 82
Verse 60: "There is no suffering for those who have..." 83
Verse 61: "In forests where others find no delight, there..." 84
Verse 62: "Even doers of good see sorrow as long as..." 85

VIRTUE

87

Verse 63: "Holding on to anger is like grasping a hot..." 89
Verse 64: "Much though he recites the sacred texts..." 90
Verse 65: "Of their own accord, they act toward..." 91
Verse 66: "If you knew what I know about the power..." 92
Verse 67: "Greed is to be slightly blamed but it is..." 93
Verse 68: "As solid rock is not shaken by the wind..." 95

Verse 69: "When a man won't listen to his..."   96
Verse 70: "Though one may conquer a thousand..."   97
Verse 71: "For a person endowed with virtue, consummate..."   98
Verse 72: "Radiate boundless love towards the..."   99
Verse 73: "If this abandoning of what is unskillful..."   101
Verse 74: "All component things in the world are..."   102
Verse 75: "Wisdom springs from meditation; without..."   103
Verse 76: "When another person makes you suffer..."   104
Verse 77: "Hold faithfulness and sincerity as first...."   105
Verse 78: "Wisdom, compassion, and courage are..."   107
Verse 79: "Humility is the solid foundation of all virtues. "   108
Verse 80: "Generosity and kind words, Conduct for..."   109
Verse 81: "Worthy persons deserve to be called so..."   110
Verse 82: "When a tree has been transplanted..."   111
Verse 83: "There is no evil like hatred..."   113
Verse 84: "One is not called noble who harms..."   114
Verse 85: "A sage does not speak in terms of..."   115
Verse 86: "Without hope of reward Provide help... "   116
Verse 87: "Foolish people follow after vanity...."   117
Verse 88: "Among the scents of sandalwood..."   119
Verse 89: "But as for a life of a hundred years..."   120
Verse 90: "If, like a shattered gong, you say..."   121
Verse 91: "Like a well-trained horse when touched..."   122
Verse 92: "Patiently shall I endure abuse as the..."   123
Verse 93: "One whose evil deeds are covered by..."   124
Verse 94: "One whose evil deeds are covered by..."   125

TRUTH   127

Verse 95: "Those who grasp at perceptions..."   129
Verse 96: "All compounded things are subject..."   130
Verse 97: "Don't go by reports, by legends, by... "   131
Verse 98: "It is wrong to cling to what you should..."   132
Verse 99: "Easily seen is the fault of others, but..."   133
Verse 100: "Whoever guides others by a procedure..."   135
Verse 101: "An error does not become truth by..."   136
Verse 102: "Once we penetrate to the Truth, we..."   137
Verse 103: "In dealing with others, be gentle and..."   138
Verse 104: "The farther away you are from the... "   139
Verse 105: "Fix your mind on truth, hold firm to... "   141

Verse 106: "Conquer the angry one by not getting..."   142
Verse 107: "Having drunk the sweetness of solitude..."   143
Verse 108: "Those who possess compassion and..."   144
Verse 109: "The one in whom there is also truth..."   145
Verse 110: "Those who know what is forbidden as..."   147
Verse 111: "If a fool is associated with a wise person..."   148
Verse 112: "As a result of the freedom they have..."   149
Verse 113: "The wise don't talk, they act..."   150
Verse 114: "There is a time for the Truth to be..."   151
Verse 115: "In our world error is continually the..."   153
Verse 116: "The oak fought the wind and was broken... "   154
Verse 117: "A monarch's carriage eventually loses... "   155
Verse 118: "Be your own light. Be your own refuge...."   156
Verse 119: "To accept some idea of truth without..."   157
Verse 120: "Do not seek the truth, only cease to..."   159
Verse 121: "If you are unable to find the truth right..."   160
Verse 122: "Every being is in search of truth, but...   "   161
Verse 123: "Fields are damaged by weeds, people..."   162
Verse 124: "But there is one taint worse than all..."   163
Verse 125: "What you seek you will find, and...   "   165

ETERNITY

Verse 126: "Every morning we are born again..."   169
Verse 127: "Whatever is of the nature to arise..."   170
Verse 128: "Neither in the sky nor in mid-ocean..."   171
Verse 129: "We all find time to do what we really... "   172
Verse 130: "If it isn't good, let it die. If it doesn't..."   173
Verse 131: "The virtuous man delights in this..."   175
Verse 132: "Long is the night to him who is awake..."   176
Verse 133: "For never does hatred cease by hatred.. "   177
Verse 134: "There is not track in the sky, and no..."   178
Verse 135: "Just as flowers open up and bear fruit..."   179
Verse 136: "Let there be nothing behind you; leave..."   181
Verse 137: "A friend loves at all times..."   182
Verse 138: "Just as vessels made of clay by a potter..."   183
Verse 139: "Thus shall you think of this fleeting..."   184
Verse 140: "I urge you not to throw away time..."   185
Verse 141: "Oh, unfathomable source of all...   "   187

Verse 142: "Nothing is born, nothing is destroyed... "   188
Verse 143: "Nothing is real but the eternal...   "   189
Verse 144: "Just understand that birth-and-death..."   190
Verse 145: "The scent of flowers does not travel..."   191
Verse 146: "And as for a life of a hundred years..."   193
Verse 147: "You hold nothing back from life; therefore...   "   194
Verse 148: "The entire world is on fire, the entire..."   195
Verse 149: "How is there laughter, how is there joy..."   196
Verse 150: "Rouse yourself! Do not be idle! Follow..."   197
Verse 151: "To learn and never think? That is delusion..."   199
Verse 152: "As water raining on a hill flows down to..."   200
Verse 153: "The doors of the Immortal are open..."   201
Verse 154: "Nothing is forever except change."   202
Verse 155: "Welcome the truth. The truth is the..."   203
Verse 156: "Heedfulness is the path to the Deathless... "   204
Verse 157: "He who has no attachment, who through... "   205

CREDITS   206

MIND

AND

BODY

VERSE 1

But to satisfy the necessities
of life is not evil. To keep the
body in good health is a duty for
otherwise we shall not be able
to trim the lamp of wisdom, and
keep our mind strong and clear.

It makes one a wiser person to meditate upon higher things, however it
is not wrong to also concern yourself with caring for the physical. Our
bodies are only vessels, yet to continue on in the world we must take care
of ourselves. Finding balance in your life is key to any type of success.

VERSE 2

An insincere and evil friend is more to be feared than a wild beast; a wild beast may wound your body, but an evil friend will wound your mind.

Beware of manipulation and the influence friends. Physical wounds may heal, but wounds to character and heart may affect the path you take in your life. Know who you are and be strong in your virtues.

VERSE 3

Be wise. Treat yourself, your mind,
sympathetically, with loving kindness.
If you are gentle with yourself, you will
become gentle with others.

Do not be too harsh on yourself. When you can calmly
understand and have patience for yourself, you will do
the same to others. The law that always remains golden
is to treat others as you also wish to be treated.

VERSE 4

By defilement of mind, beings are
defiled; by purification of mind,
beings are purified.

Greed, delusion, and hatred are either present or absent
in the mind, there is no middle point. No one is perfect,
however be conscious of your self and strive for a healthy
mind. Your mind-state can determine the quality of your life.

VERSE 5

As long as the mind does not know itself,
as long as the mind is not bright and
illuminated, the mind is not free.

Remaining in ignorance is a form of bondage. To be liberated,
remove ignorance from the mind. Awaken yourself from the
sleep of those who choose to be "of this world."

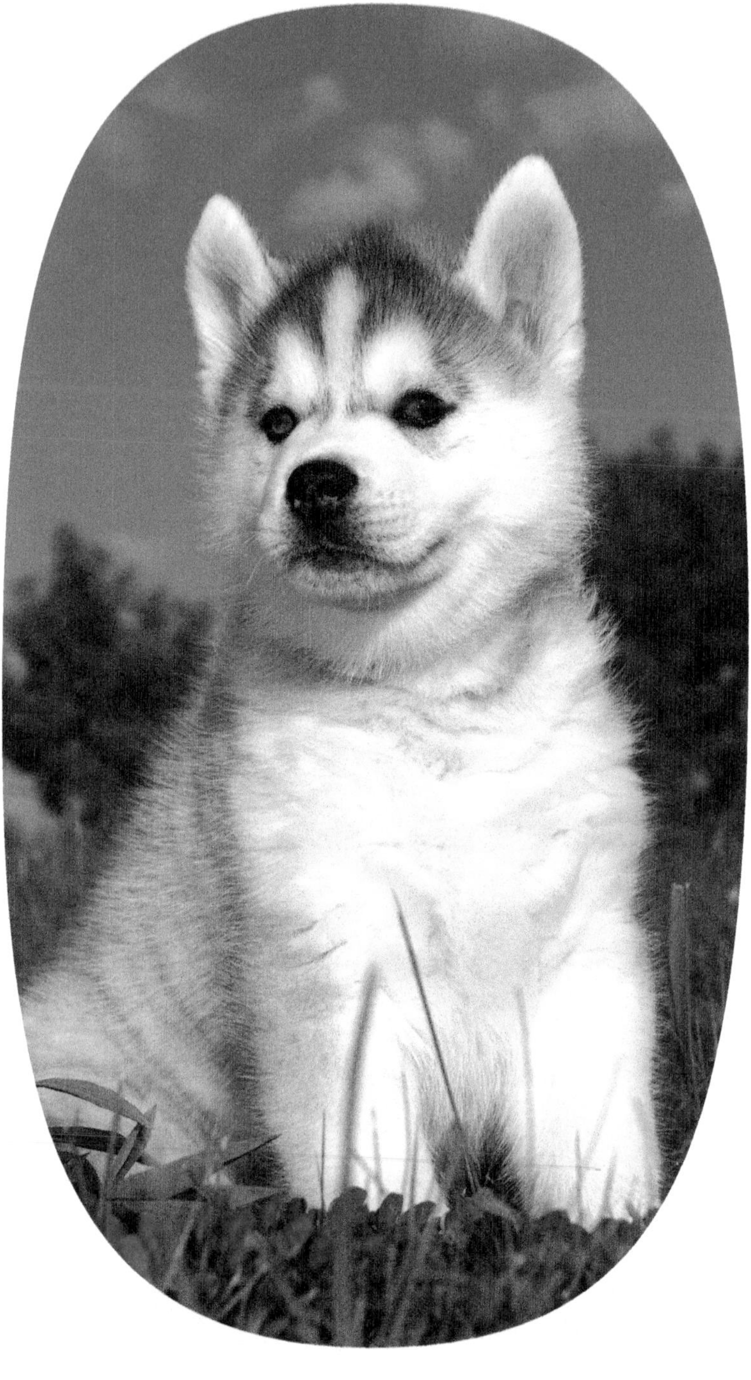

VERSE 6

To keep the body in good
health is a duty, otherwise
we shall not be able to keep
our mind strong and clear.

Mind and body are interdependent. The body must remain
healthy, for it is an instrument in the mind's quest for spirituality.
You can not sail to new, exotic seas if your ship is ailing.

VERSE 7

Think with the whole body.

Just like the mind, there is wisdom and knowledge of the body. Trust its innate instincts. Listen to every facet of information that comes to you. Your heart, your gut, your mind, and your physical body all provide unique information.

VERSE 8

Do not lose yourself in the past. Do not lose yourself in the future. Do not get caught in your anger, worries, or fears. Come back to the present moment, and touch life deeply. This is mindfulness.

It is impossible to be constantly thinking of the past and future and still get the most out of life. Focus your full attention in the present moment and connect to "the now," to increase your mindfulness and the quality of your experiences.

VERSE 9

Not the wind, not the flag;
mind is moving.

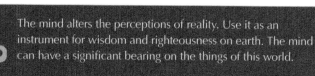

The mind alters the perceptions of reality. Use it as an instrument for wisdom and righteousness on earth. The mind can have a significant bearing on the things of this world.

VERSE 10

Buddha means awareness, the awareness of body and mind that prevents evil from arising in either.

The body and mind must be disciplined to remain focused and healthy. Guard yourself against evil and meaningless temptation. This could encompass anything from excess materialism, gossip, jealousy, greed, and more.

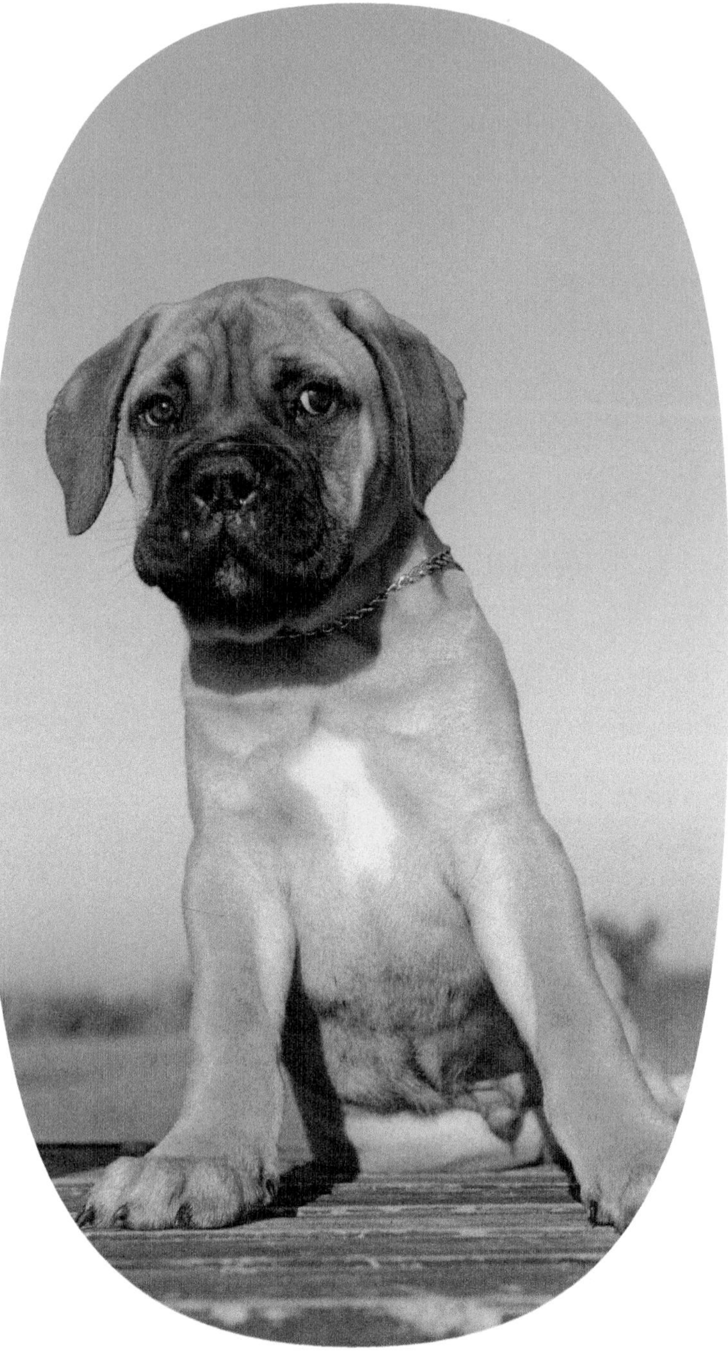

VERSE 11

Calming allows us to rest,
and resting is a precondition
for healing.

Both the mind and body must rest in order to stay healthy. Yin and yang encompass the very meaning of balance. Yin is rest, yang is movement. You cannot be balanced with just stimulation and action, but will also be unbalanced with only rest and reflection.

VERSE 12

If you want to climb a mountain,
begin at the top.

The fight is always won before it begins. Set your sights
high—not just towards your goal, but beyond it.

VERSE 13

I come to realize that mind is no other than mountains and rivers and the great wide earth, the sun and the moon and stars.

The mind is as complex and beautiful as the earth and heavens—where you choose to roam, however, will make the difference as to what you see, experience, and learn. Direct your mind to higher things, beautiful and bright destinations.

VERSE 14

It is a man's own mind, not his enemy or foe, that lures him to evil ways.

A undisciplined mind can easily be led astray by manipulation and bad influences. Take responsibility and action for yourself to know what is right.

VERSE 15

If with a pure mind a person speaks
or acts, happiness follows them like a
never-departing shadow.

Being genuine is very rare nowadays, especially
speaking and acting from the heart. Try speaking and
acting today only with pure and sincere motives,
you may be surprised at how much effort it takes.

VERSE 16

When deluded, one is called an ordinary being, but when enlightened, one is called a Buddha. This is similar to a tarnished mirror that will shine like a jewel when polished. A mind now clouded by the illusions of the innate darkness of life is like a tarnished mirror, but when polished, it is sure to become like a clear mirror, reflecting the essential nature of phenomena and the true aspect of reality.

Ignorance in the mind is always deliberate. We all have the choice to follow the path to enlightenment, yet choosing to do nothing is still making a decision. Choose better for yourself and to improve the quality of your life.

VERSE 17

The way you do anything is the way you do everything.

The integrity, the attitude, and the reflex reaction you have to anything is truly how it will be always be, unless you take steps towards betterment.

VERSE 18

If you are unwilling to make efforts to heal yourself, it will be very difficult to cure your illness. One day of life is more valuable than all the treasures of the major world system, so first you must muster sincere faith.

You cannot teach someone who does not want to be taught or help someone who's not want to be helped. If you are frustrated and feeling lost, yet do not seek any wisdom, you will not find growth. Seek and ye shall find!

VERSE 19

Control your eyes, ears, nose,
body, mind and thought. With
such control, a holy person will be
free from suffering.

Often being rash and impulsive causes great harm. Be
patient and have the strength to control yourself.

VERSE 20

Pride and indifference shroud this heart, too,
as the sun is obscured by the piled-up clouds;
supercilious thoughts root out all modesty of
mind, and sorrow saps the strongest will.

Certain attitudes can completely cut you off from
wisdom. That is why someone who is angry is blind to
facts and difficult to reason with. You can not let the
light in if something is blocking the window.

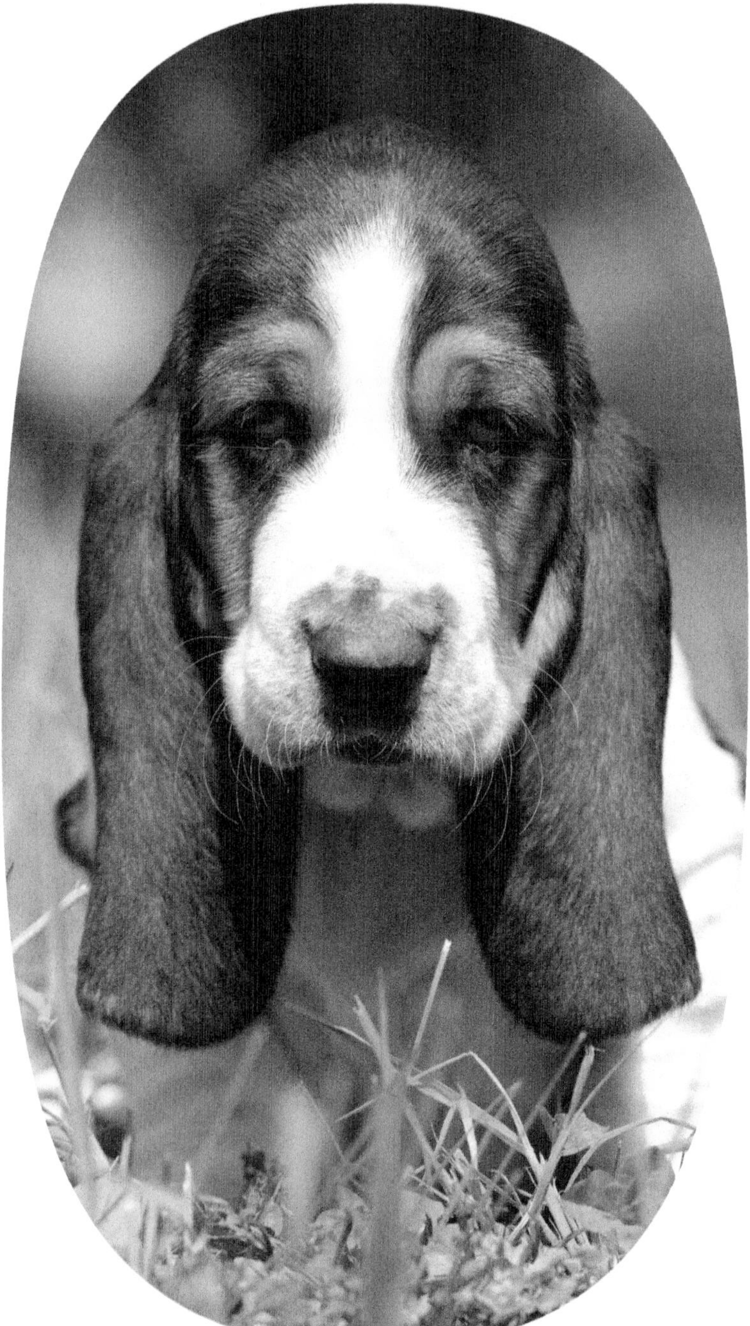

VERSE 21

Hell does not exist from its own side; the negative mind makes it up.

Hell is not just a fiery pit deep down in the basement of heaven—it is a state of mind that we deliberately open the door to. It is filled with negative emotions. Some might think this means something dramatic, yet even something as common as lying or road rage allows "hell" into the world.

VERSE 22

Like a fish taken from the water and thrown on the dry ground, our mind quivers all over in its effort to escape the dominion of Mara [the death-causer].

Fears often control peoples lives, decisions, and perceptions. Set yourself free of the unkown.

VERSE 23

Neither a mother, nor a father, nor any other relative will do to one as great a service as one's own well-directed mind.

The strongest source of peace stems from a reflective mind. Seeking advice and input from others when making a difficult choice may help sometimes, however, often you will find that deep down you already know the answers.

VERSE 24

One who has no wound on the hand may touch
poison with the hand. Poison does not affect
one who has no wound, nor does evil befall
one who does not commit.

The wound is the karmic result on the body's susceptibility
to evil. Evil only enters if there is a doorway for it. Cultivate
strength in righteous ways, and build a shield to evil.

VERSE 25

Irrigators guide the water; fletchers craft the arrow; carpenters shape the wood; good people fashion themselves.

Self-growth and development is a craft only suited for yourself, not others. You are the sculptor of yourself and it is up to you to sculpt yourself into something great.

VERSE 26

Death carries off a person
who is gathering flowers
with a distracted mind,
just as a flood carries off a
sleeping village.

It is easy to be fooled when we wish to be fooled or "asleep." When are eyes are not open, and we are simply content with routine and convenience, we make ourselves vulnerable. Open your eyes and seek wisdom with all your heart.

VERSE 27

One who has learned little grows old like a
dumb ox: flesh may increase, not wisdom.

True wisdom is found in the mind, not age.

VERSE 28

Those who, having broken free from lust, give themselves up to lust again—those who, having escaped the jungle, run back to the jungle—these ones are caught in bondage.

Repeating bad habits and giving into evils, when they are known to cause harm, is an indicator of slavery, not freedom.

VERSE 29

Let right deeds be your motive, not the fruit that comes from them.

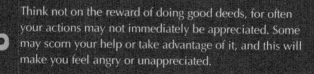

Think not on the reward of doing good deeds, for often your actions may not immediately be appreciated. Some may scorn your help or take advantage of it, and this will make you feel angry or unappreciated.

VERSE 30

Even so, an action to be done by body, speech or mind should only be done after careful reflection.

All actions have consequences. Any step you take will have a direct effect upon you and others, think of every possible outcome and make sure the choice is one you are comfortable with.

HAPPINESS

VERSE 31

I do not dispute with the world; rather it is the world that disputes with me.

Do not waste happiness by challenging the ways of the world. Instead, create a path to achieve happiness through the midst of it all. The world, in its knowledge and ways, will shape you.

VERSE 32

Better than a thousand useless words
is one useful word, hearing which
one attains peace.

Speak wisely, truthfully, and economically
to help yourself and others gain peace.

VERSE 33

There is no way to happiness,
happiness is the way.

Happiness is not a goal. There is no black and white
recipe to happiness, no marked path. Happiness is the
path. You must choose it, and stay on it.

VERSE 34

We will develop and cultivate the
liberation of mind by loving kindness,
make it our vehicle, make it our basis,
stabilize it, exercise ourselves in it,
and fully perfect it.

Kindness is the route to peace with yourself and others.
It is the foundation to grow and eventually reach
freedom from the negativity that weighs us down.

VERSE 35

Health is the greatest gift, contentment
is the greatest wealth.

The finest things of life are those which you cannot
buy—they are achieved. They are priceless. No
matter how rich in material wealth you are, you will
always be poor if you are without them.

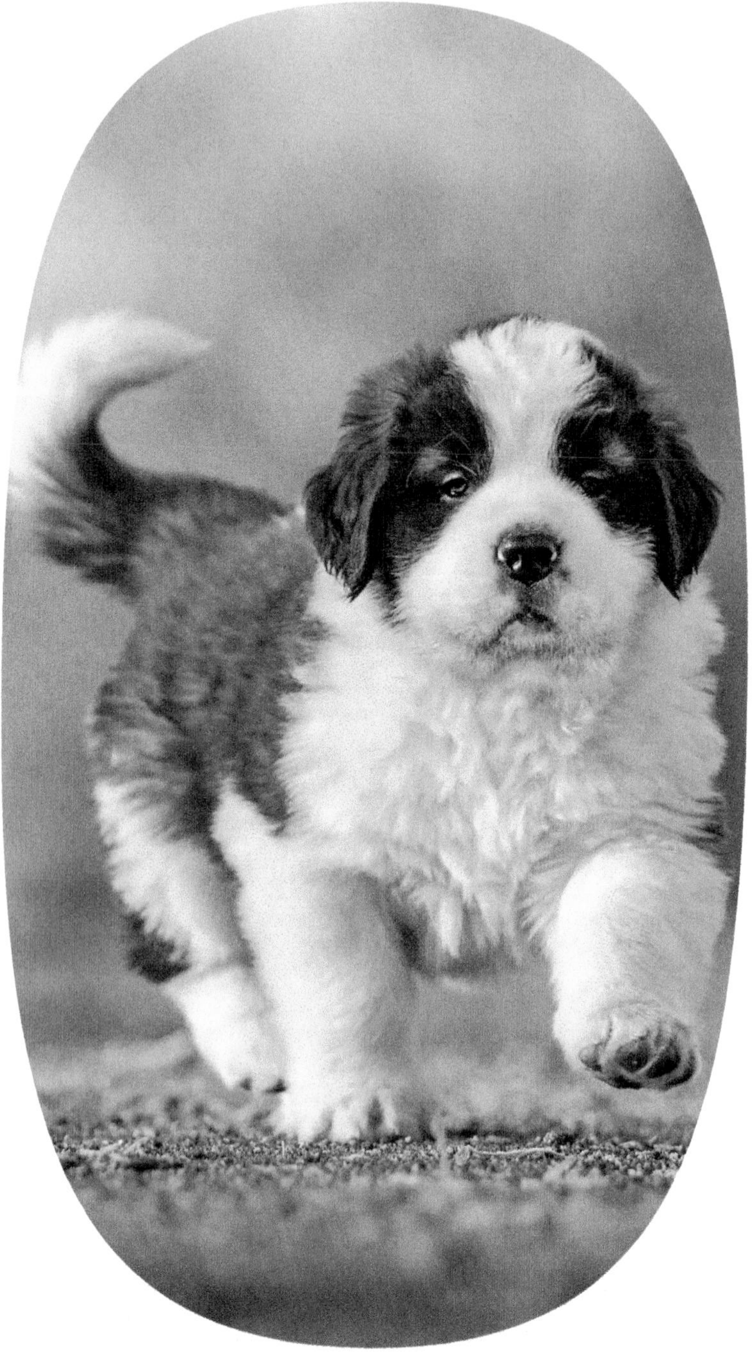

VERSE 36

The Buddha said, "Those who rejoice in seeing others observe the Way will obtain great blessing." A Sramana asked the Buddha, "Would this blessing be destroyed?" The Buddha replied, "It is like a lighted torch whose flame can be distributed to ever so many other torches which people may bring along..."

Like the flame that multiplies without being extinguished, happiness increases by being shared with those that surround you. Fellowship in a common goal is something unique and treasured that unites people.

VERSE 37

He who is provided with forbearance and loving-kindness is always lucky, honored and happy. He is also beloved and appreciated by divine and human beings.

True and honest virtues in a person will be celebrated and appreciated by those who know how valuable these are.

VERSE 38

Acquisition is the root of suffering.

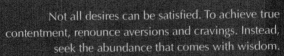

Not all desires can be satisfied. To achieve true
contentment, renounce aversions and cravings. Instead,
seek the abundance that comes with wisdom.

VERSE 39

Sometimes your joy is the source of your
smile, but sometimes your smile can be
the source of your joy.

Someone once said to smile—just smile—even if there is
no practical reason to at the moment. Try it! Smile, and
you will eventually find something to be happy about.

VERSE 40

Everyone hears only what he understands.

The close-minded only wish to hear what makes sense to them, and do not attempt to see beyond, or find the true meaning. Open you mind and heart and see things for what they are—not what you wish them to be.

VERSE 41

Letting go gives us freedom, and freedom is the only condition for happiness. If, in our heart, we still cling to anything—anger, anxiety, or possessions—we cannot be free.

Renouncement is the precept of freedom that gives way happiness. By remaining slaves to desires, emotions, and the past, neither freedom nor happiness can be achieved. Material possessions are chains that bind us to the ground, instead of letting us fly.

VERSE 42

The ocean of suffering is immense, but if you
turn around, you can see the land. The seed
of suffering in you may be strong, but don't
wait until you have no more suffering
before allowing yourself to be happy.

Suffering can be a black hole, there will never be a limit to
it, but make the choice not to get pulled in and lost inside.
Instead, taste what you must and have the strength to turn
away and choose happiness again.

VERSE 43

If you understand, you will suffer less, and you will know how to get to the root of injustice.

To suffer less, remain within the bounds of wisdom and reason, away from emotions like fear or anger. Only by thinking clearly is it possible to fix the problems that harm you and the world.

VERSE 44

You yourself must strive. The Buddhas only point the way.

It is not enough to just read and learn the teachings of Buddha. Buddha cannot grant Nirvana. Only through personal dedication and work can enlightenment be reached.

VERSE 45

All those who suffer in the world do so because of their desire for their own happiness. All those happy in the world are so because of their desire for the happiness of others.

Thinking of personal happiness only is selfish, while thinking upon yours and that of the world is selfless. No man is an island, and one can not be happy alone.

VERSE 46

If a man does what is good,
let him do it again; let him
delight in it: happiness is the
outcome of good.

The universe works through cause and effect. Animals do something good and feel the immediate effects of pride and affection from their owners. This is the same with humans and the universe. The effect of a good action breeds more good in the world.

VERSE 47

He who knows that all things are his
mind, that all with which he meets are
friendly, is ever joyful.

Greet thoughts and circumstances with positivity.
Life is what you make of it, and what you get out of
it is directly proportional to what you put in.

VERSE 48

They are happy indeed who own nothing at all;
Those with highest knowledge own nothing at all.
See how people who own things are afflicted,
Bound to others by their obligations.

Ownership binds you to attachment and attachment
binds you to the servitude of your desires that
prevents freedom and, consequently, happiness.

VERSE 49

The one who walks in the company of fools
suffers a long way. Company with fools,
as with enemies, is always painful.
Company with the wise is happiness,
like meeting with kinfolk.

The wise, knowing evil does not cause happiness, follow
the path of goodness. Fools purposefully follow the path
of evildoing. If you are influenced by the wise you will be
happy, but if you are influenced by fools you will suffer.

VERSE 50

There is no fire like passion, there is no evil like hatred, there is no pain like this bodily existence, there is no happiness higher than peace.

You can not be at peace if you are not happy, yet you can not be happy without being at peace. Seek what matters most.

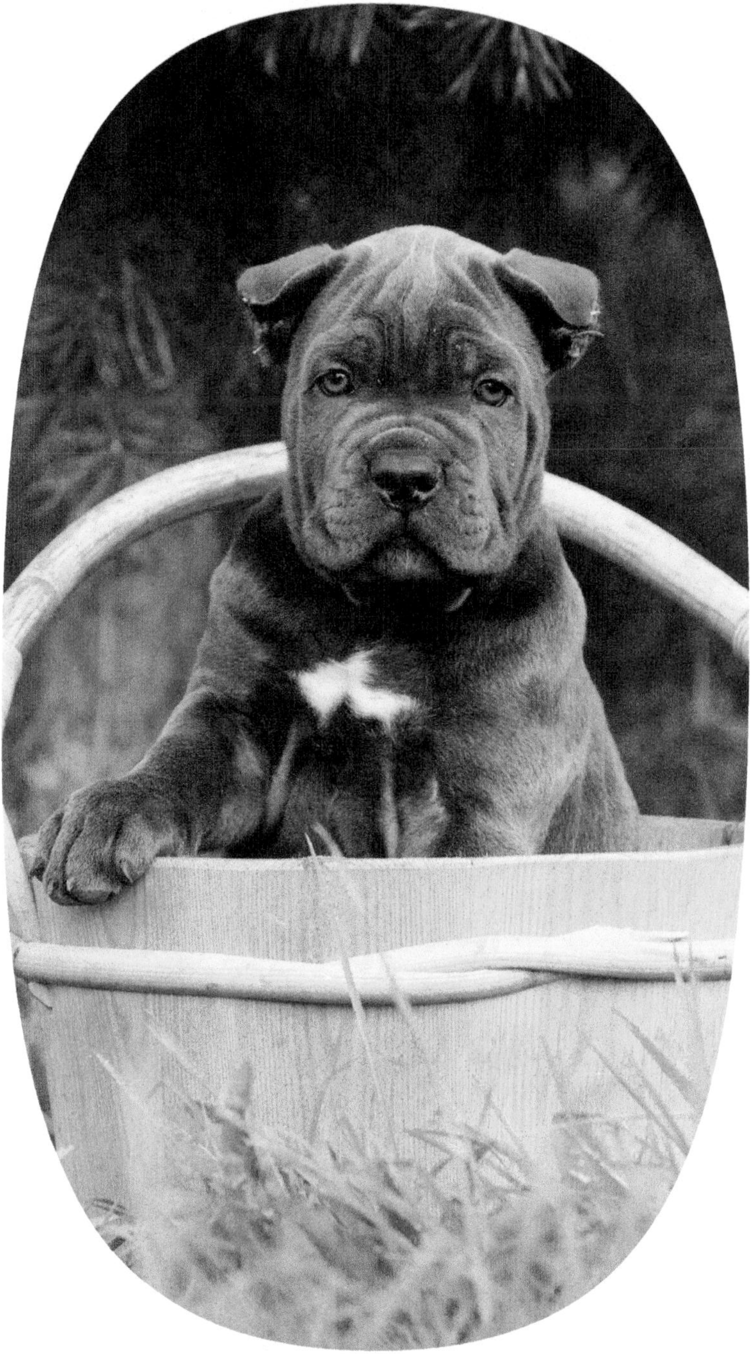

VERSE 51

We live happily indeed when we
are not hating those who hate
us! Among those who hate us
let us dwell free from hatred!

Although it is tempting to hate those that wish to cause harm, hatred
only breeds unhappiness. It is better to focus on self-happiness than
fall into the same unhappiness of others. You can not control the
opinions and attitudes of others, only yourself.

VERSE 52

From pleasure comes grief, from pleasure comes fear. The one who is free from pleasure knows neither grief nor fear.

When desires are satisfied, states of pleasures are reached. But desires are never satisfied and tempt morally wrong actions. To renounce worldly pleasure is to renounce the possibility of evil, unfulfillment, and dissatisfaction.

VERSE 53

Those who, seeking their own happiness,
punish beings who also long for happiness,
will not find happiness after death [in the
next rebirth].

Happiness will never be reached at the expense of
another. Selfishness will never lead to happiness.

VERSE 54

Mules are good if trained, and so are noble horses and great elephants, but humans who train themselves are better still.

It is easier to train a puppy than to train yourself, unfortunately. Self-control is a crucial skill to achieve goodness and happiness.

VERSE 55

Be not thoughtless, watch your thoughts!
Draw yourself out of the evil way, like an
elephant sunk in the mud.

Guard the mind and be attentive of all that occurs in the
world around you. Without self-realization, it is easy to
deviate from the path of good. Evil ways are like ditches in
the road, falling in can harm you and hold you back.

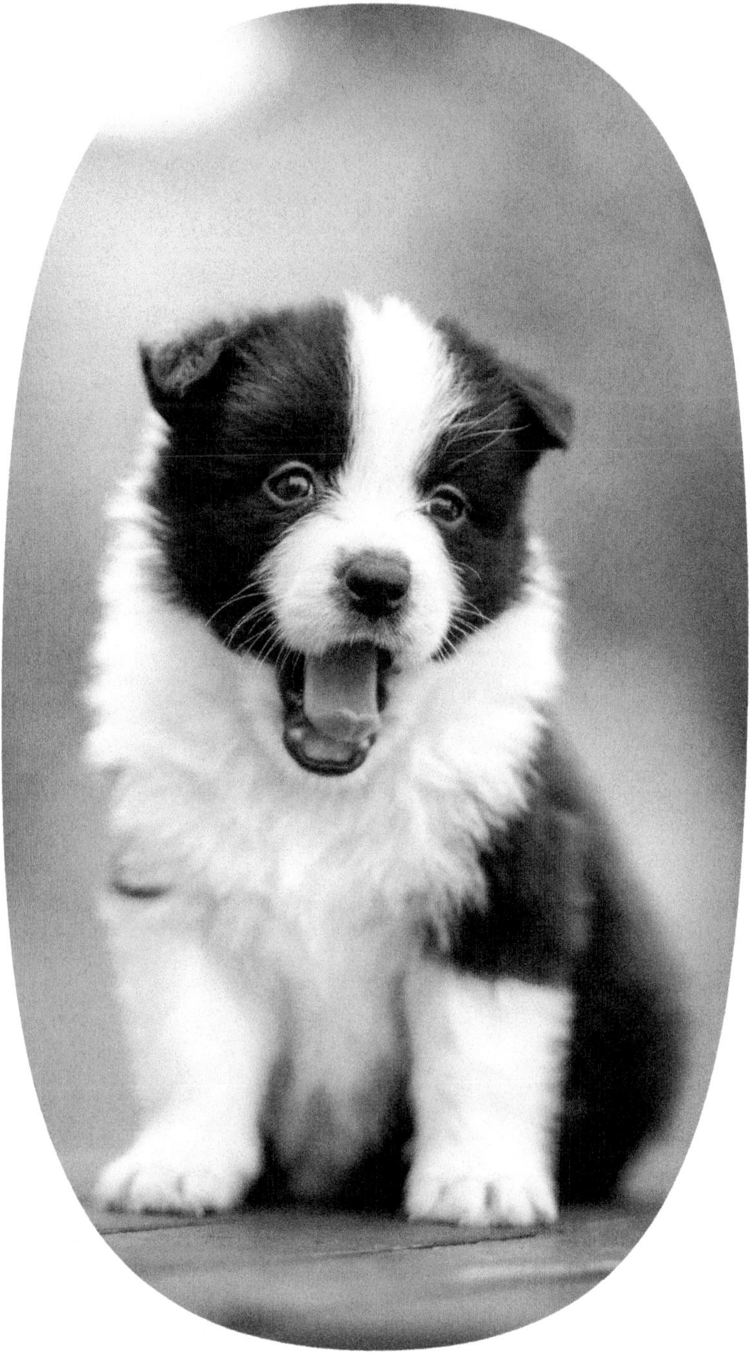

VERSE 56

But whoever overcomes this fierce, poisonous thirst—in this world, that person is difficult to be conquered, and that person's sufferings fall off like water dropping from a lotus leaf.

In a world surrounded by corruption, make an effort to grow with goodness, like the lotus that blossoms albeit growing in mud.

VERSE 57

Those who are slaves to passion follow the stream of desires, as a spider runs down the web it has made. When they have ceased to do this, at last they make true progress, free from cares and leaving all pains behind.

Desires only trap you in a never-ending web of servitude to them. These desires will never allow you to reach happiness—surrendering them will eliminate suffering.

VERSE 58

No, a deed is well done if one does not repent it, and if the reward is happiness and good cheer.

Goodness comes without guilt. Although the results of a good deed may not be immediate, good karma will nonetheless be come back to you.

VERSE 59

The good renounce everything. The virtuous do not prattle with a yearning for pleasures. The wise show no elation or depression when touched by happiness or sorrow.

Life is a circle of everything—birth and death, good times and bad, sadness and jubilance. Everything shall pass and come again in due course.

VERSE 60

There is no suffering for those who have finished their journey, foresworn grievous desires, and freed themselves fully from all bonds.

Happiness will come from enlightenment, when all desires and attachments are left behind. You have nothing left in the way to disturb the peace in your heart and mind.

VERSE 61

In forests where others find no delight, there they will know delight. Because they do not look for pleasure, they will have it.

Those who are wise do not need to seek after pleasure and amusement. They find it, and delight in its simplicity, wherever they are.

VERSE 62

Even doers of good see sorrow as long as their good deeds have not ripened; but when their good deeds have ripened, then do the doers of good see happiness.

Results of kind actions may not be visible at first, but their effect will cause happiness once set in motion.

VIRTUE

VERSE 63

Holding on to anger is like grasping
a hot coal with the intent of
throwing it at someone else; you
are the one who gets burned.

Anger is a vice with double consequences. Although
it may hurt another, it will always hurt you also.

VERSE 64

Much though he recites the sacred texts, but acts not accordingly, that heedless man is like a cowherd who only counts the cows of others—he does not partake of the blessings of the holy life.

To be virtuous, knowledge and speech are insufficient. Credence must be demonstrated through agency and action. Practice what you preach.

VERSE 65

Of their own accord, they act toward themselves as a dear one would act toward a dear one; thus they are dear to themselves.

Be kind to yourself. Although it is ethical to extend concern to others, granting yourself compassion is not an act of selfishness, but of protection of your well-being. You can not help and love others if you need help and love yourself.

VERSE 66

If you knew what I know about the power of giving, you would not let a single meal pass without sharing it in some way.

Generosity demonstrates both compassion and kindness. It's importance breeds happiness in both the giver and receiver.

VERSE 67

Greed is to be slightly blamed but it is slow to change. Hatred is to be greatly blamed but it is quick to change. Delusion is to be greatly blamed and it is slow to change.

Only by understanding that these three poisons are the root of suffering can these vices begin to be eliminated.

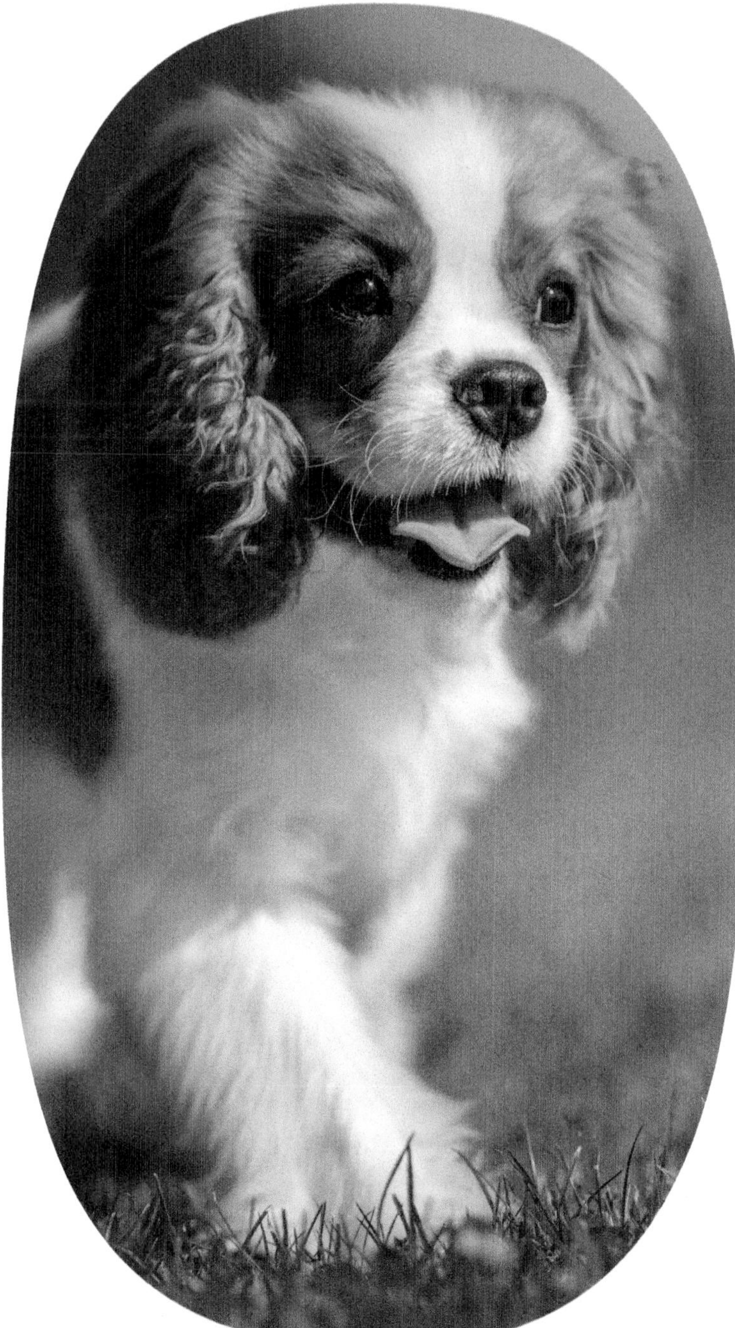

VERSE 68

As solid rock is not shaken by the wind, so the wise are not shaken by blame or praise.

Do not allow external circumstances determine your emotions. If you are wise, you will already know if you merit praise or criticism.

VERSE 69

When a man won't listen to his conscience,
it's usually because he does not want advice
from a total stranger.

Know yourself. Listen to your inner voice until it
grows strong and loud. Your higher conscience
will guide you towards what is right.

VERSE 70

Though one may conquer a thousand times a thousand men in battle, yet he indeed is the noblest victor who conquers himself.

Self-conquest is the most victorious conquest. Once you have conquered yourself, you are the master of yourself and your destiny.

VERSE 71

For a person endowed with virtue, consummate in virtue, there is no need for an act of will, 'May freedom from remorse arise in me.

Often we feel negative emotions out of insecurity of ourselves or situations. By nature, a person complete with virtue will be at peace, confident in the strength of their actions and mind.

VERSE 72

Radiate boundless love towards the entire world—above, below, and across—unhindered, without ill will, without enmity.

There is not one being on this earth who does not need love. Spread it to all you can reach. Genuine goodwill and love are foundations of peace on earth.

VERSE 73

If this abandoning of what is unskillful were conducive to harm and pain, I would not say to you, 'Abandon what is unskillful.' But because this abandoning of what is unskillful is conducive to benefit and pleasure, I say to you, 'Abandon what is unskillful.'

Let go of what does not help you accomplish your goals. If it does not release you from suffering, it contributes to it. What does not aid you to grow, holds you back.

VERSE 74

All component things in the world are changeable. They are not lasting. Work hard to gain your own salvation.

Our perceptions are constantly in flux. Although these perceptions distort reality and may affect thoughts, continue to strive towards enlightenment.

VERSE 75

Wisdom springs from meditation; without meditation wisdom wanes. Having known these two paths of progress and decline, let a man so conduct himself that his wisdom may increase.

Meditation's very nature is reflection. Through meditation, you are able to open the nature of your mind, reflect on the things that have passed and surrender to be at peace.

VERSE 76

When another person makes you suffer, it is because he suffers deeply within himself, and his suffering is spilling over. He does not need punishment; he needs help. That's the message he is sending.

Compassion is a virtue not easy to abide by in the face of hatred and suffering. Look at suffering from a new angle, the victim as one that needs healing and compassion.

VERSE 77

Hold faithfulness and sincerity as first principles.

All other virtues are connected, and each grows from each other, especially these two. Hold these fast to yourself and you will grow in a righteous path.

VERSE 78

Wisdom, compassion, and courage are the three universally recognized moral qualities of men.

Morality is found in those that demonstrate love of knowledge, attentiveness, and sensitivity to indignity. Choose to follow these traits in daily conduct and you can count yourself among the righteous.

VERSE 79

Humility is the solid foundation of all virtues.

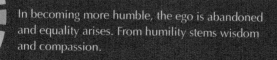

In becoming more humble, the ego is abandoned and equality arises. From humility stems wisdom and compassion.

VERSE 80

Generosity and kind words, Conduct for others' welfare, Impartiality in all things These are suitable everywhere.

Do not be nervous or unsure of yourself. You will always act properly when you act in these virtues. Treat beings equally and kindly, and spread compassion in all the ways possible.

VERSE 81

Worthy persons deserve to be called so because they are not carried away by the eight winds: prosperity, decline, disgrace, honor, praise, censure, suffering, and pleasure. They are neither elated by prosperity or grieved by decline.

Outside circumstances should not determine you as a person. Circumstances will always change around you, have the strength to make yourself remain constant and steadfast.

VERSE 82

When a tree has been transplanted, though fierce winds may blow, it will not topple if it has a firm stake to hold it up. But even a tree that has grown up in place may fall over if its roots are weak.

Be true and dedicated to the virtues and the moral compass you possess. Foundations in righteousness will make you strong against the winds of misfortune.

VERSE 83

There is no evil like hatred. And
no fortitude like patience.

No matter the evil acts that are thrown at you, do not fret.
Patience allows for a clear mind that will help solve the obstacles
presented, hatred will only keep you further from happiness.

VERSE 84

One is not called noble who harms living beings. By not harming living beings one is called noble.

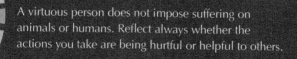

A virtuous person does not impose suffering on animals or humans. Reflect always whether the actions you take are being hurtful or helpful to others.

VERSE 85

A sage does not speak in terms of being equal, lower or higher. Calmed and without selfishness he neither grasps nor rejects.

Still your passions and control ego. Abstaining from greed and demonstrating compassion is a true sign of wisdom.

VERSE 86

Without hope of reward Provide help to others. Bear suffering alone, And share your pleasures with beggars.

Give without expecting reward. Do not hand out the poison of suffering, but gifts.

VERSE 87

Foolish people follow after vanity. Wise people guard vigilance as their greatest treasure.

Being knowledgable is a great gift, one that you can use to your advantage and that of others. Vanity only serves one person, and makes one a prisoner to it.

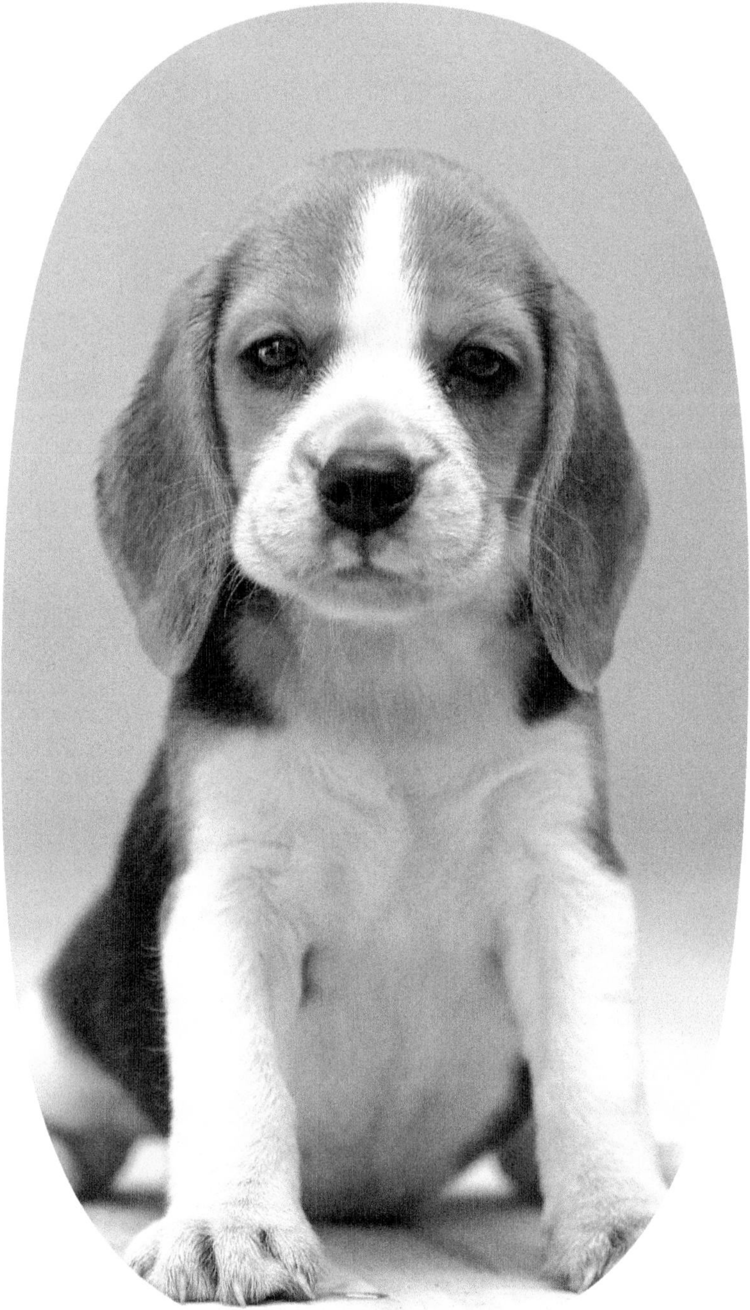

VERSE 88

Among the scents of sandalwood, rosebay, the blue loyus, and jasmine, the perfume of virtue is the best.

Nothing is as sweet and pleasurable as good virtue. A good moral compass and kindly disposition are positive traits that people admire and like to be around.

VERSE 89

But as for a life of a hundred years lived viciously and unrestrained—a life of one day of virtue and self-control is better.

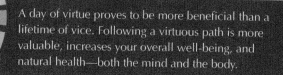

A day of virtue proves to be more beneficial than a lifetime of vice. Following a virtuous path is more valuable, increases your overall well-being, and natural health—both the mind and the body.

VERSE 90

If, like a shattered gong, you say nothing harsh, then you have reached nirvana; anger is not known in you.

By rising above passions, like anger, you can attain wisdom. The virtue of patience brings you self-control, and leaves the harshness of impulsive ways behind.

VERSE 91

Like a well-trained horse when touched by a whip, be eager and active to do good. By faith, by commitment, by vigor, by attention, by insight into the law, and by virtuous behavior, you will cast off the burden of misery.

Goodness requires discipline. To eliminate suffering, perseverance and commitment are important to maintain virtuous behavior.

VERSE 92

Patiently shall I endure abuse as the elephant in battle endures the arrow sent from the bow: for the world is ill-natured.

Even the strong and innocent are victims to the cruelty of the world. Through frustration and agitation, more harm can emerge. Through patience and forbearance, pain lessens.

VERSE 93

One whose evil deeds are covered by good
deeds brightens up this world, like the
moon when freed from the clouds.

No one is perfect, and evil deeds can be redeemed. It is
never too late to practice kindness and compassion.

VERSE 94

One whose evil deeds are covered by good deeds brightens up this world, like the moon when freed from the clouds.

Spread boundless love to all beings as if they were your own. In treating all as equals, we spread loving kindness throughout.

TRUTH

VERSE 95

Those who grasp at perceptions and views go about butting their heads in the world.

There is only truth in the world, clouded by perspectives. Stubbornness of opinions will only result in conflict. Instead seek the truth, making no conclusions until it arrives fully.

VERSE 96

All compounded things are subject to vanish.
Strive with earnestness!

Everything that is formed is inconstant. All material will fade. In life we must follow the truth with conviction.

VERSE 97

Don't go by reports, by legends, by traditions, by scripture, by logical conjecture, by inference, by analogies, by agreement through pondering views, by probability, or by the thought, 'This contemplative is our teacher.'

Believe nothing for its own sake. Reason and common sense are not enough to determine truth. Instead, look to your own experiences and observations of wisdom.

VERSE 98

It is wrong to cling to what you should not believe in, or to fail to ask about a truth you should seek.

Do not remain stagnant in your life, following the path of lost and blind. Whatever you seek is what you find. Seek nothing and you will find nothing.

VERSE 99

Easily seen is the fault of others, but one's own fault is difficult to see. Like chaff one winnows another's faults, but hides one's own, even as a crafty fowler hides behind sham branches.

We are more critical of others because we approach their faults from a different perspective. It takes more effort to see the truth within ourselves, especially since we hide it with our perceptions.

VERSE 100

Whoever guides others by a procedure that is nonviolent, and fair is said to be a guardian of truth, wise and just.

Truth is not spread by aggression, it is spread through justice. That is what makes a good leader.

VERSE 101

An error does not become truth by reason of multiplied propagation, nor does truth become error because nobody sees it. Truth stands, even if there be no public support. It is self-sustained.

A lie that no one catches is still a lie. Those who have integrity will uphold what is true and right even if acting the opposite is never discovered.

VERSE 102

Once we penetrate to the Truth,
we are freed from everything.
Only peace remains.

Freedom of doubt grants peace and there is no doubt in truth. Once we discover what is true, the right decision can be taken in tranquility.

VERSE 103

In dealing with others, be gentle and kind.

The sad truth is that every person is going through something. We will always be tested and put through challenges in life. Be kind to others, as you can be an instrument of hope in their lives.

VERSE 104

The farther away you are from the truth, the more the hateful and pleasurable states will arise. There is also self-deception.

Do not deceive yourself by the pleasures that tempt the senses, abstain from these pleasures and you shall arrive at the truth. While sensation is based on perception, truth is based on reality.

VERSE 105

Fix your mind on truth, hold firm to virtue, rely on loving kindness, and find your recreation in the Arts.

Truth can guide you towards virtue, compassion, and the expression of creativity.

VERSE 106

Conquer the angry one by not getting angry;
conquer the wicked by goodness; conquer
the stingy by generosity, and the liar by
speaking the truth.

When encountering people that do not practice goodness,
do not mimic their actions. Conduct yourself with honesty,
patience, kindness, and charity and perhaps they will
mimic yours.

VERSE 107

Having drunk the sweetness of solitude
and also the sweetness of tranquility,
one becomes free from fear and
wrongdoing while drinking the
sweetness of the joy of truth.

Many repair themselves and find peace in
solitude. One can be free from distractions,
leaving only your true inner thoughts.

VERSE 108

Those who possess compassion and wisdom,
who are just, speak the truth, and take
responsibility for themselves—those the
world holds dear.

If you treat others equally, spread kindness and truth, and
hold responsibility, those around you will do the same.
Your actions will multiply and inspire others.

VERSE 109

The one in whom there is also truth, goodness, gentleness, self-control, and moderation, the one who is steadfast and free from impurity—that one is rightly called an elder.

Age does not determine the label, "elder." The mind and not the body is what determines wisdom.

VERSE 110

Those who know what is
forbidden as forbidden, and
what is not forbidden as what
is not forbidden—such people,
embracing the true doctrine,
enter the good path.

Those that see the truth as it is and are not deviated by their
perceptions are able to follow the morally right path.

VERSE 111

If a fool is associated with a wise person for an entire lifetime, that fool will perceive the truth as little as a spoon perceives the taste of soup.

Being surrounded by someone wise does not make you wise. Wisdom comes for accepting the truth and correcting negative actions and thoughts.

VERSE 112

As a result of the freedom they have attained through knowledge of the truth their thoughts are peaceful, their words are peaceful, and their deeds are peaceful.

Knowledge can sometimes be a blessing, and sometimes a curse. The same goes for wisdom, however it usually endows the bearer with a certain peace and strength.

VERSE 113

The wise don't talk, they act.

Imagine a world where no one could speak or write. In this kind of world, all that really can speak are actions, which matter most. Words are wind, as George R.R. Martin says.

VERSE 114

There is a time for the Truth to be revealed to you. If you don't believe it then, it is your loss.

There will come be a time to face truth. Be prepared, because you may finally see it, yet find it unpleasant or unexpected, and choose to remain blissfully ignorant. Gain the wisdom you can, and search for enlightenment.

VERSE 115

In our world error is continually the handmaid and pathfinder of Truth; for error is really a half-truth that stumbles because of its limitations; often it is Truth that wears a disguise in order to arrive unobserved near to its goal.

The pursuit of bettering yourself, higher thinking, and attaining knowledge is not always straight. In fact it is never straight, and rarely ever easy. Do not be discouraged, however, as giving up is the only certain way to fail.

VERSE 116

The oak fought the wind and was broken,
the willow bent when it must and survived.

We accept change more easily when we are younger,
and avoid like the dentist's office when we grow older.
It is something that we can never avoid, and should
try to embrace.

VERSE 117

A monarch's carriage eventually loses its shine and, similarly, the body decays. Enlightened beings have told us that truth and goodness live on.

Deep down we know what truly matters: love, goodness, truth, and enlightenment, yet so many choose to keep themselves in the dark. Choose to chase after what really matters—and what lasts.

VERSE 118

Be your own light. Be your own refuge. Confide in nothing outside of yourself. Hold fast to Truth that it may be your guide. Hold fast to Truth that it may be your protector.

A great songwriter once wrote "we come alone, and alone we die." So, instead of looking for fulfillment and reassurance somewhere else, find it inside of yourself.

VERSE 119

To accept some idea of truth without experiencing it is like a painting of a cake on paper which you cannot eat.

All that is told to us cannot be believed to be true. To determine truth we must eliminate deception by experiencing it firsthand.

VERSE 120

Do not seek the truth, only cease to cherish your opinions.

Once attachment to your perceptions and ego is abandoned, the truth will come freely. Often, we ignore the truth because we fear our mistakes.

VERSE 121

If you are unable to find the truth right where you are, where else do you expect to find it?

Some think they need to be somewhere in the wilderness to get in touch with their true self, or with a guru in a foreign continent to seek truth and enlightenment. But truly you can find it right where you are. There is nowhere it can hide.

VERSE 122

Every being is in search of truth, but small fears go on preventing you.

Many people are scared of failure, but even more are afraid of success.

VERSE 123

Fields are damaged by weeds, people are damaged by delusion. Therefore, a gift bestowed on those who are free from delusion brings great reward.

Those that mistake the false for the truth cannot be gifted with the eternal law. To follow Buddha, one must acknowledge the truth.

VERSE 124

But there is one taint worse than all other: Ignorance is the greatest taint. O walkers of the way! Throw off that taint and become taintless altogether!

The sins of the world will only be revealed once we overcome ignorance and embrace the truth. Once we arrive at the truth, we can rid ourselves of our sins.

VERSE 125

What you seek you will find, and
what you ignore you lose.

What we choose to let into our lives is what will enter
in. Be conscious of what you want and what you
choose to seek, as they can be very different.

ETERNITY

VERSE 126

Every morning we are born again. What we do today is what matters most.

It is never to late to be the person you want to be. Every morning you have the chance to better yourself—begin today. There is no end to how great you can be.

VERSE 127

Whatever is of the nature to arise, all that
is of the nature to cease.

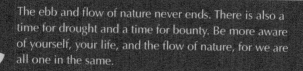

The ebb and flow of nature never ends. There is also a
time for drought and a time for bounty. Be more aware
of yourself, your life, and the flow of nature, for we are
all one in the same.

VERSE 128

Neither in the sky nor in mid-ocean, nor by entering into mountain clefts, nowhere in the world is there a place where one may escape from the results of evil deeds.

Evil is not found in the air, nor can it be found in the trees or rain—but in the minds of men. So, always take the path of love and goodness, because whatever you allow into your heart will follow.

VERSE 129

We all find time to do what we really want to do.

The truth is, time is relative; even if we had an eternity of it, it is up to us to use it wisely.

VERSE 130

If it isn't good, let it die. If it doesn't die, make it good.

What we choose to do and make of this life is the only thing we can both take with us and also leave behind.

VERSE 131

The virtuous man delights in
this world and he delights in the
next; he delights in both.

Living in the moment is all well, however being aware of higher
influences and greater things will bring more meaning to your life
than worldly life. The greatest dreamers of our age are "not of this
world," as the phrase goes.

VERSE 132

Long is the night to him who is awake; long is
a mile to him who is tired; long is life to the
foolish who do not know the true law.

This quote references biblical language, which usually
classifies fools as those who choose to forsake what is good
and righteous. When you are suffering through something,
it will seem greater depending on your mind state.

VERSE 133

For never does hatred cease by hatred at any time. Hatred ceases by love. This is the eternal law.

Just as we see in today's world, almost nothing is ever accomplished by fighting fire with fire. You cannot crush hate with hate, only with love and solidarity.

VERSE 134

There is not track in the sky, and no recluse outside (the Buddha's dispensation). There are no conditioned things that are eternal, and no instability in the Buddhas.

All things that are conditioned are part of creation. All animals, humans, nature, are governed by a higher law. Our hearts beat, we breathe, live, and eventually die—we can't control our natures because we are creation.

VERSE 135

Just as flowers open up and bear fruit, just as the moon appears and invariably grows full, just as a lamp becomes brighter when oil is added.

There are certain things that make one grow, or become better and brighter. All of these examples demonstrate growth and, just as nature does, how doing good and striving for what is right will expand us.

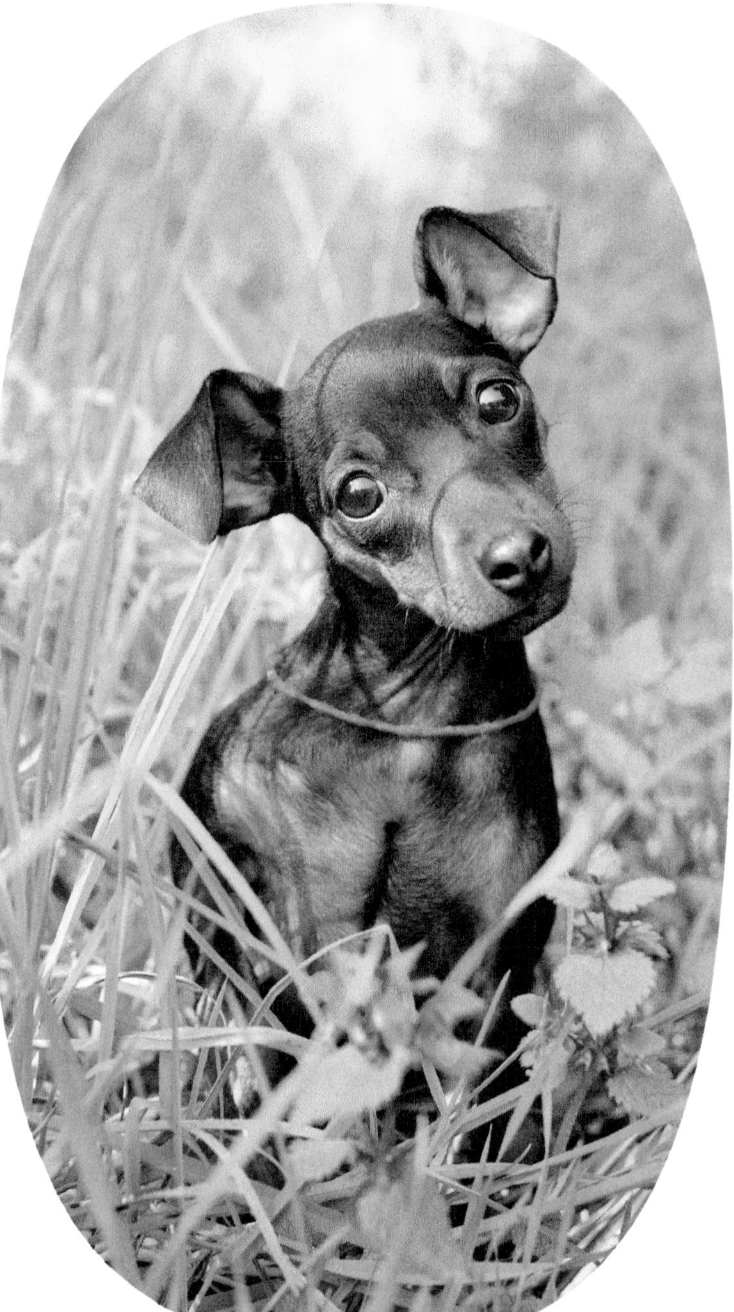

VERSE 136

Let there be nothing behind you; leave the future to one side. Do not clutch at what is left in the middle; then you will become a wanderer and calm.

There is much to be said for living in the moment, but there is more to it. This quote demonstrates the importance of letting go and getting rid of baggage, as it will free you and release stress more than you know.

VERSE 137

A friend loves at all times.

Sincere friendship does not choose when and where to show itself, but remains always. Love is also a choice that, if true, does not waver.

VERSE 138

Just as vessels made of clay by a
potter all have breaking as their end,
so is the life of mortals.

A change of perspective can allow you to see time, the
universe, and the meaning of things in a different way.

VERSE 139

Thus shall you think of this fleeting world:
A star at dawn, a bubble in a stream,
A flash of lightning in a summer cloud,
A flickering lamp, a phantom, and a dream.

Our time on earth is short and it is the small, beautiful details that we will ultimately remember—the special moments. Look for those around you now.

VERSE 140

I urge you not to throw away time, for
it's swift as an arrow, fast as a stream.
Distraction is entirely due to lack of
concentration; stupidity and blindness are
caused by lack of true knowledge.

We are the only species that really measures time,
yet also the only kind that wastes it so much. Live
consciously, not blinded by what is put in front of you.

VERSE 141

Oh, unfathomable source of all things!...Hidden deep but ever present!

It is easy to get lost in mundane life. Unfortunately, routine often blinds us, steals the magic, and takes away our ability to see and think in an enchanted state of mind.

VERSE 142

Nothing is born, nothing is destroyed. Away
with your dualism, your likes and dislikes.
Every single thing is just the One Mind.

This quote urges you to detach from "black or
white" thinking, from possessions, ego, and from
the modern mind-state.

VERSE 143

Nothing is real but the eternal. Nothing will last but the eternal.

Despite what religion you follow, the power that governs this world never changes.

VERSE 144

Just understand that birth-and-death is itself nirvana. There is nothing such as birth and death to be avoided; there is nothing such as nirvana to be sought. Only when you realize this are you free from birth and death.

The fear of death and excitement (or fear) of birth are common but, as this quote explains, they are simply part of the circle of life. Do not react to birth or death in the typical way, but with acceptance.

VERSE 145

The scent of flowers does not travel against the wind, nor that of sandalwood, rosebay, or jasmine. But the fragrance of good people travels even against the wind. Thus a good person pervades the universe.

No matter the resistance and evil that goodness is up against, it will always make itself known and prevail. Just like a small flower blooming in the middle of a concrete city.

VERSE 146

And as for a life of a hundred years living without seeing the eternity—a life of one day seeing eternity is better.

The quality of your life far outweighs the duration. What is the purpose of a long life if you are living it blindly, without intention, materialistically, and without higher thinking? It is unfulfilled.

VERSE 147

You hold nothing back from life; therefore you are ready for death, as a person is ready for sleep after a good day's work.

Live with passion, bravery, and intention now. That way, at the end, you will have no "what if's."

VERSE 148

The entire world is on fire,
the entire world is burning.

The world is full of desire. These desires and conditions are temporary and always changing; often, if not always, these desires destroy us. Buddhism teaches detachment, which is the only way to find true contentment.

VERSE 149

How is there laughter, how is there joy,
as this world is always burning? Why
do you not seek a light, you who are
shrouded in darkness?

We often think we know what will make us happy in this modern age, yet we destroy and blind ourselves through ignorance. Christian scripture says, fittingly, that people die from lack of knowledge.

VERSE 150

Rouse yourself! Do not be idle! Follow the law of virtue! The virtuous rest in bliss in this world and the next.

Many find it easier to forgo the effort. The reward of being virtuous, however, can not only bring peace to you on this earth, but always.

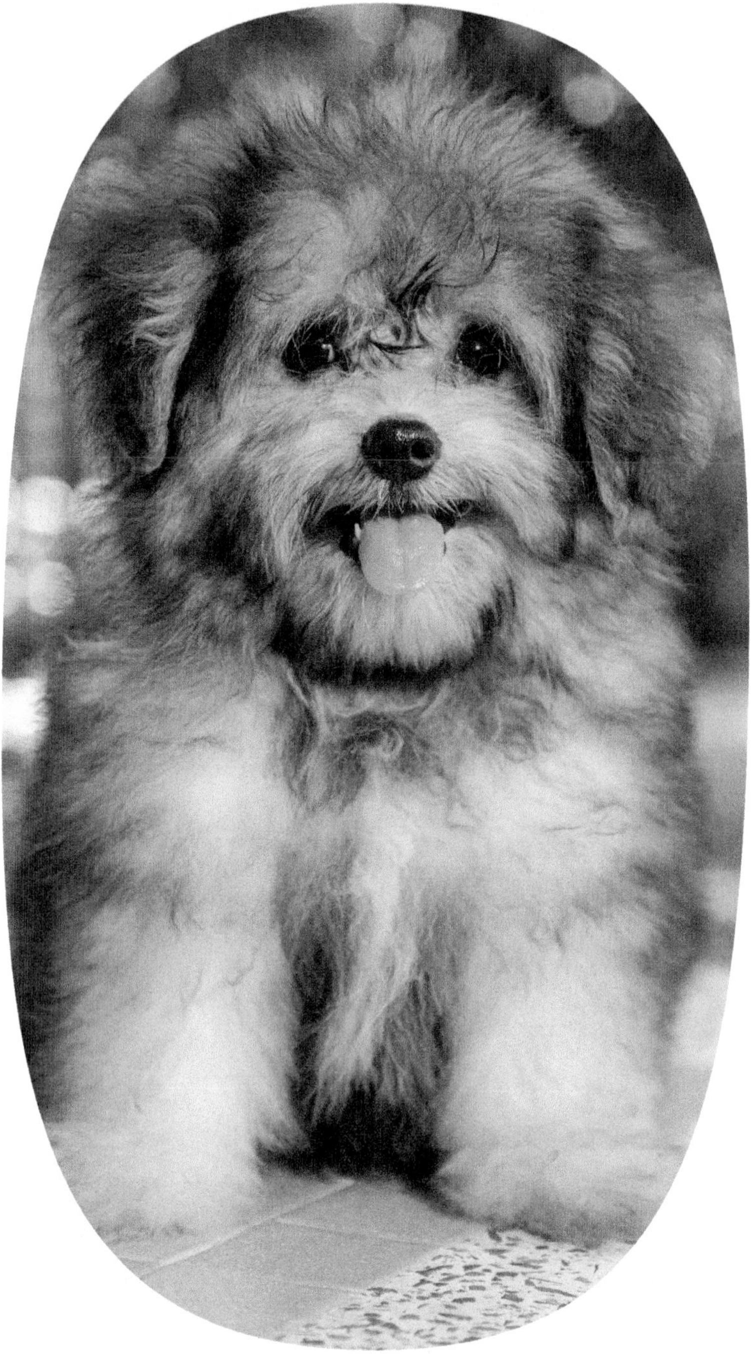

VERSE 151

To learn and never think? That is delusion. But to think and never learn? That is perilous indeed!

Seek knowledge, but do not merely take it into your mind—meditate upon the wisdom you acquire. It is not enough to know a thing, without deeply thinking upon it yourself. Students never grow into teachers without this important step.

VERSE 152

As water raining on a hill flows down to the valley, even so does what is given here benefit the dead.

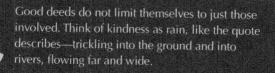

Good deeds do not limit themselves to just those involved. Think of kindness as rain, like the quote describes—trickling into the ground and into rivers, flowing far and wide.

VERSE 153

The doors of the Immortal are open. Let those who can hear respond with faith.

Humans have the potential to achieve enlightenment if they follow the path of Buddha with openness and willingness.

VERSE 154

Nothing is forever except change.

The one thing we can always count on is change. Many find it intimidating, others exciting. Something that can usually be said about it, however, is that it often coincides with progress and growth.

VERSE 155

Welcome the truth. The truth is the immortal part of the mind.

What kind of thoughts occupy your mind today?

VERSE 156

Heedfulness is the path to the Deathless. Heedlessness is the path to death. The heedful die not. The heedless are as if dead already.

In choosing to be awake, however, although you carry the burden of wisdom, you are now truly alive, as the wisdom and virtue in your heart and mind is immortal.

VERSE 157

He who has no attachment, who through
perfect knowledge is free from doubts
and has plunged into the Deathless—
him do I call a holy man.

Detachment has always been one of Buddhism's foremost
teachings. Doing this allows you to focus on bettering yourself
and seeking holiness. Being deathless does not meant not
dying, but to die to yourself and the things of this world.

CREDITS

All Photos from Shutterstock

Cover: Irina Kozorog

p. 10: phoebe
p. 12: michaeljung
p. 13: Hannamariah
p. 14: Chrislofotos
p. 15: minik
p. 16: Dmitry Kalinovsky
p. 18: Scorpp
p. 19: Cynthia Kidwell
p. 20: anetapics
p. 21: Jim Larson
p. 22: cynoclub
p. 24: Marcel Jancovic
p. 25: Nagel Photography
p. 26: otsphoto
p. 27: Fnsy
p. 28: otsphoto
p. 30: Mila Atkovska
p. 31: dragon_fang
p. 32: Lurin
p. 33: Waldemar Dabrowski
p. 34: Zuzule
p. 36: Sergey Lavrentev
p. 37: YamabikaY
p. 38: PCHT
p. 39: FiledIMAGE
p. 40: Dora Zett
p. 42: Mary Rice
p. 43: otsphoto
p. 44: Sergey Lavrentev
p. 45: Grigorita Ko
p. 48: Dora Zett
p. 50: Grigorita Ko

p. 51: JLSnader
p. 52: Grigorita Ko
p. 53: feeling lucky
p. 54: Grigorita Ko
p. 56: Dora Zett
p. 57: Dora Zett
p. 58: sw_photo
p. 59: sw_photo
p. 60: otsphoto
p. 62: Grigorita Ko
p. 63: Stephen Dukelow
p. 64: Grigorita Ko
p. 65: Nadiia Diachenko
p. 66: Bianca Grueneberg
p. 68: Grigorita Ko
p. 69: Helen Sushitskaya
p. 70: Natalia Fedosova
p. 71: Shirsendu1995
p. 72: Utekhina Anna
p. 74: Christian Mueller
p. 75: PCHT
p. 76: Smit
p. 77: Sergey Lavrentev
p. 78: xkunclova
p. 80: djile
p. 81: Vera Zinkova
p. 82: ANNA TITOVA
p. 83: Sergey Lavrentev
p. 84: Grigorita Ko
p. 85: Sbolotova
p. 88: otsphoto
p. 90: Grigorita Ko
p. 91: otsphoto
p. 92: Y_P

p. 93: Christian Mueller
p. 94: Morrison Media
p. 96: Natalia Fedosova
p. 97: Kate Grishakova
p. 98: Victoria Rak
p. 99: Sarune Kairyte
p. 100: otsphoto
p. 102: Yevgen Romanenko
p. 103: Vivienstock
p. 104: Margarita Zhuravleva
p. 105: Dmitriy Karmanov
p. 106: Denis Tabler
p. 108: Chee Hao Lee
p. 109: Helen Sushitskaya
p. 110: Runa Kazakova
p. 111: Tatyana Kuznetsova
p. 112: Grigorita Ko
p. 114: Melounix
p. 115: Morrison Media
p. 116: Natasha Ray
p. 117: Didkovska Ilona
p. 118: Sigma_S
p. 120: Waldemar Dabrowski
p. 121: xkunclova
p. 122: December35
p. 123: Rabsh
p. 124: nayton rosales
p. 125: Djordje Novakov
p. 128: JustUsForUs
p. 130: Revaphoto
p. 131: BiggsJee
p. 132: Eudyptula
p. 133: Sigma_S
p. 134: ANURAK PONGPATIMET

p. 136: otsphoto
p. 137: dezy
p. 138: TMArt
p. 139: Nikolai Tsvetkov
p. 140: Sandra Huber
p. 142: ANURAK PONGPATIMET
p. 143: ANURAK PONGPATIMET
p. 144: Natalia Fedosova
p. 145: alarich
p. 146: Photo-SD
p. 148: Eve Photography
p. 149: rokopix
p. 150: icarmen13
p. 151: Rabsh
p. 152: Bachkova Natalia
p. 154: Evgeniia Shikhaleeva
p. 155: Zanna Holstova
p. 156: mikeledray
p. 157: Evgeniia Shikhaleeva
p. 158: Evdoha_spb
p. 160: TOM KAROLA
p. 161: CHATTIP
p. 162: Ezzolo
p. 163: Aumsama
p. 164: ANURAK PONGPATIMET
p. 168: Anneka
p. 170: Lars Christensen
p. 171: Utekhina Anna
p. 172: Dmitry Kalinovsky
p. 173: cynoclub
p. 174: Kristen Kahne
p. 176: PardoY
p. 177: Tatiana Katsai
p. 178: 91172573

p. 179: Ewais

p. 180: PozitivStudija

p. 182: Sergey Lavrentev

p. 183: Natalia Fedosova

p. 184: PCHT

p. 185: Grigorita Ko

p. 186: Nataliia Melnychuk

p. 188: Grigorita Ko

p. 189: Sbolotova

p. 190: Grigorita Ko

p. 191: ANURAK PONGPATIMET

p. 192: Dorottya Mathe

p. 194: Annette Shaff

p. 195: Sbolotova

p. 196: Bachkova Natalia

p. 197: Smit

p. 198: LittleDogKorat

p. 200: Verbitskaya Juliya

p. 201: Tsuguliev

p. 202: Eve Photography

p. 203: Yana Kiselyova

p. 204: michaelheim

p. 205: Ricantimages

The Zen of Dogs and Cats

ISBN 978-1633530485
PRICE US$12.70
TRIM 5X8

ISBN 978-1633535237
PRICE US$11.52
TRIM 5X8

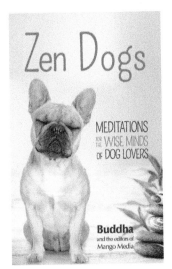

ISBN 978-1633535213
PRICE US$11.52
TRIM 5X8

CPSIA information can be obtained
at www.ICGtesting.com
Printed in the USA
BVOW10s0929011217
501646BV00001B/3/P